ISBN 9798647216199
First English Edition 2020

Translation: Sofia Kougianou, MA in Translation Studies, University of Birmingham

Proofreading: Melinda Bende, MA in English Language and Literature, University of Szeged

Edited: Reader Symeon Campbell

Cover design: Chrysostomos Tromboukis, B.A. www.chrysostomo.wordpress.com

Publisher: Archangels Publications
Retail orders: www.archangelsbooks.com
Wholesale orders: archangelspublications@gmail.com

"There is one great thing about man that I admire: His control of his passions" (Al. Carrel).

Archim. Vassilios Bakoyiannis

BATTLES & PASSIONS
Anger, Hatred, Envy

"Archangels Publications"

PART III.
E N V Y

EPILOGUE

APOSTLE PAUL

*"But you yourselves are to put off all these: anger, wrath, malice..." (*Col. 3:8)

"Put on the whole armor of God... For we do not wrestle against flesh and blood...take up the whole armor of God, that you may be able to withstand in the evil day, and having done all, to stand...

*Stand therefore, having girded your waist with truth, having put on the breastplate of righteousness, and having shod your feet with the preparation of the gospel of peace above all, taking the shield of faith with which you will be able to quench all the fiery darts of the wicked one. And take the helmet of salvation, and the sword of the Spirit, which is the word of God." (*Eph. 6:11-17)

St Paul by Rublev

INTRODUCTION

Bodily instincts (passions) are hunger, sleep, etc. They have one common purpose, the biological sustenance of man. (They are called blameless passions). The instinct of hunger leads man to feel the lack of food. Man stays alive by eating. He eats so that he may live, not live to eat. The same thing applies to the instinct of thirst, etc.

Man also has spiritual blameless passions (instincts): zeal, anger, wrath, fear, and sorrow. Like the passions of the body, which serve to help us survive physically, the purpose of the spiritual passions is to sustain us to survive spiritually. We have the passion of anger to feel anger against evil and, by doing so, to cut ties from it. We also have jealousy; to be jealous of the good and then imitate it. In addition, we have fear, to make us humble, and by doing that, we manage to survive spiritually, etc.

God has placed our mind at the highest point of our body, in the forehead, to oversee all our passions. Scripture calls it *"the Master of the passions"* (4 Mac. 1:7).

Our mind is the governor of our passions. It should move and set them in the right motion.[1] Nevertheless, because their fulfillment is accompanied by pleasure, it is hard for us who are lustful, to say "no" to something that gives us pleasure. As a consequence, reason is being carried away by the impulse of pleasure, and it becomes the slave of passions. We do not eat to live, but we live to eat.

Thus, we do not use our passions for survival but our self-destruction. Instead of contributing to our salvation, they become a means of our condemnation.

The devil is a virgin, but he is still the devil. Most Christians try to avoid sinning bodily while spiritually they are boiling over with anger, hatred, envy, etc. The spiritual passions *"are worse*

---

[1] An animal has the same bodily instincts, but the instincts of man are under the control of the mind. Between the personality of man and his instincts, logic intervenes. This difference makes man a man and an animal an animal. That is why David would say: *"Wretched man, while he had the honour to have logic, he did not use it, but he lowered himself to the level of mindless animals and became just like them"* (Ps. 49:12-13).

and more serious than the bodily passions."[2] These spiritual passions don't create a feeling of remorse, in reference to the bodily passions, and lead to repentance. They mess up the soul more than the bodily passions do without our realizing it.[3] They are so dangerous that they *"even lead into a condition that is like the demons."*[4] The fearful expressions *"woe to you"* (Mt. 23:13-33), that Jesus applied to the Pharisees who were slaves of spiritual passions!

When Adam was in paradise, he had the same passions of body and soul but in the right form. E.g., he ate in the glory of God; he was angry in the detriment of evil; he hated the evil, etc. and by doing so, he elevated himself spiritually. But he sinned, and his passions changed direction. After the fall, he ate to fill his stomach, and he was angry with his brother, he hated his brother, etc. He downgraded spiritually speaking. And we have inherited this false function of the passions. Our mission is to reset them to their initial function,

---

[2] St John of Damascus, a miraculous and soul-saving talk from the Philokalia v. 2nd
[3] Abba Kassius, Conversations with the father of the desert, v. I. page 286. (Greek edition)
[4] St John of Damascus. Ibid

the one before the fall.

"Evil and passion do not exist by nature in the humans, because God is not the creator of evil and passions."[5] Which means that *"the image of God did not disappear, but it has been blurred, just as the mirror."*[6] Thus, the clear nature that Adam had before the fall is alive inside us. It is simply concealed by the distorted nature that his sin created. It groans because it is oppressed.

It groans particularly when we do things against its virtuous wish, when we are angry with our brother, when we hate, envy, or do him wrong. On the contrary, it rejoices when we do things according to its wish. When we forgive our brother, we love him, and we do good to him.

It is true that when we love or forgive our brother, we feel differently from how we feel when we hate or do not forgive him, let alone the consequences that this has on the health of our soul and body. [7]

---

[5] St John of the Ladder, Step 26, On discernment of thoughts, passions and virtues, 41. (All quotations from Holy Fathers have been freely translated by the author from Ancient Greek into Modern Greek).
[6] St Athanasious, Homily against Greeks, , 8. P.G. 25, 16
[7] More: On the Epilogue. 1. Passions and Illnesses

St John Chrysostom

"We admire the King seated on his throne, wearing the sumptuous crown and gown. But man is much more admirable for creating the mind of the King; he put his on his throne, and from up there he governs his passions, by putting up his head a shiny, spiritual crown" *("If your Enemy is Hungry"* **4 P.G. 51: 177)**

St Matthew

PART I
ANGER

1. *"Whoever Is Angry..."*

The Lord said: *"whoever is angry with his brother without a cause shall be in danger of the judgment"* (Mt. 5:22).

-Who gets angry *"without a cause"*?

-Nobody. We all have a specific reason that irritates us, particularly.

-Does this mean that we are innocent in front of Christ because we have a reason?

The part of *"without a cause"* did not exist in the original Scripture. It was added by the copyists that did not comprehend the spirit of the Bible. Because the Bible wishes to cut us completely from the sources of anger. In other words, the Lord did not say, *"whoever is angry with his brother without a cause shall be in danger of the judgment"* (Mt. 5:22), but He just said, *"whoever is angry with his brother shall be in danger of the judgment."*[8]

---

[8] Abbas Cassian. Conversations with the Fathers of the Desert, vol. II. "Hetoimasia" p. 483. By the opportunity:

And that is how it is. Because the Lord mentioned it when He was talking about the commandment *"thou shalt not kill"* to burn the roots of murder, and by extension, anger to the ground. He said: *"You have heard that it was said to those of old, 'You shall not murder, and whoever murders will be in danger of the judgment.' But I say to you that whoever is angry with his brother shall be in danger of judgment"* (Mt. 5:21-22).

As if He was saying: When you get angry with your brother, you are dangerous. In that moment, when you are not yourself, you might end up committing murder. But even if you do not commit murder, you have made a start by being angry. Your mind has been filled up with thoughts against your brother. Your thoughts are going to 'give birth' to feelings of hatred against your brother in your heart. And if you get angry again,

---

Until the time of typography (15th century), the copyists copied texts, and mistakes were made. Such mistakes were made while copying the Holy Bible. The Ecumenical Patriarchate set up a special three-member commission to "review" the New Testament. Thus, in 1904 the text of the Testament was adopted, which we have today. It seems that for this particular passage (Mt 5:22) the Commission did not have the ancient manuscripts in mind that Abbas Cassian did. This does not ruin the message of the Scriptures, *"that Jesus is the Christ, the Son of God, and that believing you may have life in His name"* (Jn 20:31).

your hatred will only increase and have consequences on your relationship between you and the person you hate.

Thus, *"get rid of the anger"* (Eph. 4:31). But if you feel angry, *"the sunset should not find you enraged"* (Eph. 4:26), be brothers again as soon as possible, so that hatred does not grow roots in your soul.

The Ladder of Divine Ascent

2. *"Be Angry, and Do Not Sin"*
(Ps. 4:4)

"Be angry, and do not sin." says the Bible. It says another thing too: *"Cease from anger, and forsake wrath"* (Ps. 37:8).[9] On the one hand, it allows us to be angry, and on the other hand, it prohibits anger completely. So what is true after all?

"By nature, there is anger against the snake (the evil) *inside us, but we tend to use it against our brothers."*[10] In other words, we have anger for one very specific purpose: to turn it against sin. Thus, *"Cease from anger, and forsake wrath"* means: Do not get angry with your brother, while *"Be angry and do not sin"* means, be angry with sin itself.

---

[9] "Wrath" in the language of the Church means pain, sorrow. *"For there* (during the destruction of Jerusalem) *will be great distress in the land and wrath upon these people"* (Lk. 21:23). *"For our deliverance from all affliction, wrath, danger and necessity"* we pray in our Church. *"What wrath found us?!"*, our fathers would say when they were facing difficult days.
[10] St John of the Ladder, Step 26, On discernment of thoughts, passions and virtues, B. 41.

The Lord, in his parable of the Great Supper (Lk. 14:16-24), illustrates the host that gets enraged (Lk. 14:21) because his guests said "no" to him by using cheap excuses. The host's anger did not turn against the guests but against the bad choice that the guests made (Lk. 14:18-20). How could they have understood their mistake if the host had not been angry about it?

And in the parable of the royal wedding (Mt. 22:1-14), the Lord describes the King as being angry; *"he was furious"* (Mt. 22:7). For the same reason, his guests refused to be present at the wedding of his son by using cheap excuses. (Mt. 22:5). Again: How could they have understood their mistake if the host had not been angry about it?

"Now the man Moses was very humble, more than all the men who were on the face of the earth" (Num 12:3). For this reason, every time Israelites were against him, he faced them with peace. But when Moses felt that he had to show his anger, he would do it. When he saw them bowing in front of a calf, Moses got so angry that he broke the holy stones that he had received from God. *"So it was, as soon as he came near the camp, that he saw the calf and the dancing. So Moses' anger became hot,*

and he cast the tablets out of his hands and broke them at the foot of the mountain" (Ex. 32:19).

Here the situation is similar: the anger was not against his Israelite brothers but against their rebellion against God.[11] How would they have been able to understand their big sin if they had not seen this mild man, Moses, get angry to the extent of smashing the holy stones that he had received from the hands of God?!

And because the anger of Moses was against sin, and not against his brothers, his mind was sparkling clean from thoughts of hatred. The only things that he felt towards his sinful brothers were love and sympathy. This then means that when we get enraged at our brothers, our mind is getting bombarded by thoughts of hatred and revenge for what they did to us. This is what Saint Paul means by saying: *"do not seek for revenge my dear but leave the rage aside"* (Rom. 12:19) [12]

---

[11] If we are not able to understand that Moses got angry over the rebellion and not with his compatriots it is because we only know to get angry with our brothers. When we get cleansed of our passions, we will also be able to get angry over sin and not with our brothers.

[12] More: St John Chrysostom, Homily 16th on the Gospel of Matthew 7. P. G 57, 248.

Pantocrator, Sinai

3. The Sinful Anger

We have a discussion with a faithless, and they mock our faith. We get angry, and we reply with rage. Why do we get angry? Is it because we feel that our ego is attacked or because they mock Christ? If we examine ourselves, we will realize that the first is true. [13] *"If you insult your brother and get angry, it is your passion that gets satisfied."*[14]

And when we satisfy our passion, we feel relieved that we expressed ourselves. And we have the illusion (fake!) that this relief was from Christ because we think that we defended Him.
In addition:

This relief becomes food for our passion, and as a result, the passion increases, and as it increases, it seeks for its food, its satisfaction. Thus, every time that we get sinfully angry, pretending that it is for the good of our brother, we become more and more malevolent! *"It is not right to de-*

---

[13] Yes! We do not love Christ, or at least we do not love Him as we should. He says, *"If you love Me, keep My commandments"* (Jn. 14:15). And one of His commandments is that we should not be angry with our brother (Matt. 5:22). Why don't we keep it?!

[14] Gerontikon. Abba Macarius, i7

23

stroy your house in order to build (if you succeed) *the house of the neighbour.*"[15] *"You do not have to lose your soul in order to save others."*[16] Therefore, as St Basil the Great says, *"direct your anger towards the murderous devil! Be sympathetic to your brother, because if he insists on sin, he will be delivered with the devil to the eternal fire!"* [17]

Again, St Basil says: *"The soldier, when he is in front of his King, does not show his anger."*[18] If he shows his anger, it is a sign of disrespect and pride. Thus:

When the greater is angry with the smaller, it is different from when the smaller is angry with the greater.

When the grandpa is angry with his grandchild, it is different from when the grandchild gets angry with his grandpa.

When a father is angry with his child, it is different from when the child gets angry with his father.

---

[15] Evergentinos. Vo. II. Case 49. Chapter 5th Abba Isaac the Syrian
[16] Gerontikon. Abba Macarius, i7
[17] Against the Anger, 6 P. G 31, 369
[18] Terms at Length, Question 127, P.G. 31, 1168.

When a priest gets angry with a common man, it is different from when a common man is angry with a priest.

When a high priest is angry with a monk, it is different from when a monk is angry with a high priest.

Getting angry among friends is different from getting angry in front of many martyrs.

St Luke

4. Anger: the Mirror of the Soul

"For out of the abundance of the heart his mouth speaks" (Lk. 6:45). It means: When we fill a container with water. The container gets filled and overflows. What overflows is the leftover. Our heart is a container. The rest that is much more is what is hidden inside us.

But why does man talk out of the leftover, and he does not speak out of his whole heart?

A good (humble) man hides the greatness of his heart, and he does not show much.

A bad person hides its impurity (because he is afraid that he might be accused). But inside him, there is a mess. God is aware of the mess, but the bad person does not take Him into account.[19]

However, when he gets angry, he loses control of himself (he is out of himself), and he shows his evilness, hidden in his heart. *"I saw people inflamed by the rage of their anger and somehow 'vomited' their long-hidden hatred."*[20] You can hear the enraged person say things unheard be-

---

[19] St John Chrysostom, Homily 42 on the Gospel of Matthew, 1 P.G. 57: 452

[20] St John of the Ladder. Step 8, on freedom from anger and on meekness, 18

fore, as a mother insulting, cursing her child. And once she is calm again, questioning herself: *"What happened to me? What did I do?"* [21]

And what happens when a person who has a pure heart gets angry? He will pour his heart out, as well. But he will not use insults! Can you imagine Saint Paisios using hurtful words?

Conclusion: if the container of our heart is full of good "material," the leftover that comes out of our mouth will be pure. *"A good man out of the good treasure of his heart brings forth good things"* (Mt. 12:35). If the container of our heart is full of evil "material," the leftover that comes out of our mouth will be evil. *"And an evil man out of the evil treasure brings forth evil things"* (Mt. 12:35).

---

[21] These words that this mother said in anger do not characterise her because she was "out of herself". Thus, we have to disregard what everyone says in anger! Even if a priest rejected Christ in his anger, he would not "loose" his priesthood. (St Symeon the Archbishop of Thessaloniki. "All his works" Part IV. Question 38. "Rigopoulou's Publications". Thessaloniki, p.368).

5. Anger: Temporary Madness

When anger works, the mind is *"out of service!"* And when the "mind is out of service," a man can do many "crazy" things! *"He who is angry is possessed by madness and does these things."* [22] That is why anger is called *"temporary madness."* [23]

Let's see how St Basil the Great describes the "foolish" behavior of an angry man. He writes:

"The moment when rage expels reason and takes over the soul, it distorts the man completely and annihilates him because he does not have reason anymore.

He sharpens his teeth and attacks like pigs do. His look is paranoiac, full of fire.

His veins become pulled and pumped. His voice becomes rough. Confused and rather incomprehensible words come out of his mouth without any coherence; unarticulated shouts! We have to deal with uncontrollable tongues, mouths without limits, that is why they emit insults, mockeries, accusations, and many other forms of rage.

In that moment, he does not have relatives. Just like a stream that overflows and carries away eve-

---

[22] On Acts 31, 4 P.G. 60, 232
[23] St Basil. Against Anger, 1. P. G. 31, 356

rything, when one gets angry, they carry away everyone and everything. They do not show respect to elderly people, honest people, relatives, anybody!

The brother forgets the brother; the father forgets the child. He raises his hand against his brother; he kicks him even in the most intimate parts of the body. Nothing is able to stop the rage of his soul, not even fire or knife. This is what possessed people do! [24]

And we should be as afraid of the enraged people as we are of the possessed". [25]

By the way, it would be of use if during our breakdown somebody could film us so we could watch with our own eyes how we master self-control!

---

[24] Against the Anger, 2. P.G. 31, 356-7
[25] St John Chrysostom. Homily 15,2 to Ephesians P.G. 62, 107-8

"You cannot find a greater proof of love than to offer your life for the sake of your brother. Thus, if you listen to somebody that says something against you and you try not to reply alike, or if you suffer injustice and you bear it without seeking revenge, you offer your life for your brother" (Gerontikon. Abbas Poemen, 135).

St Basil The Great

6. When the Other Person Is Angry

You sit quietly in your office. All of a sudden, your colleague comes to your office out of his mind and "attacks" you. What will you do? Imitate him? Follow his madness?

"Did your fellow insult you? And you are insulting God, who is your Lord! And you are insulting Him once too many times! How is it possible for a servant to insult his Lord?" [26]

"With his insults against you, he has already closed Heaven's door, because as Saint Paul says, 'those who insult shall never inherit God's Kingdom.'" On the contrary, your silence opens the road to the Heaven's Kingdom, because: *"he who will endure will be saved finally."* [27]

"It is a huge loss for your enemy to see you untouched, invincible against his wild attacks that shoot you while being enraged. He will be stigmatized as an angry, insulting person while you will be a magnanimous, cheerful, and mild person. He will regret what he did and said, you, on the contrary, will not". [28]

---

[26] St John Chrysostom, Homily 21,1 on the statues P.G. 49, 198-9
[27] St Basil the Great, Against Anger, 4 P. G. 31, 360-1
[28] St Basil the Great, against anger, 4 P. G. 31, 360-1

"Do not let your enemy be your teacher. Do not fall to his level. Do not imitate his passion. Do not be jealous of what you hate. Do not cure evil with evil." [29] "Anger is like a raging fire that needs wood in order to grow. If you do not throw wood, it will fade out. Anger by itself is weak. There has to be someone to 'nourish' it, in order to grow." [30] Do not be that someone!

"A soft answer turns away wrath, but a harsh word stirs up anger" (Prov. 15:1).

If you wish to fade out the fire that has been broken out in the other person's soul (and you should), watch your mouth. Do not use irritating, rough words but rather mild, soft words that make the fire fade out.

If you do so, your brother will calm down. And you discourage him from acting worse. Be a savior; be his benefactor. And you shall receive mercy from the Lord. And in case your brother keeps being angry, despite your mildness, you are still the winner.

«*"I want to be a martyr for Christ," said a monk to a holy father. And the holy father replied: "If in a*

---

[29] St Basil the Great, against the anger, 3. P.G. 31, 357
[30] St John Chrysostom, on Acts 31,4 P.G. 60, 232

difficult moment you can endure your fellow brother, that equals with the torture of the three children in the kiln!"» [31]

---

[31] Evergetinos, v. II. Case 37. Chapt. I,8.

St John Chrysostom

7. When You Are Angry Too

St John Chrysostom: *"You go to a feast and see someone drunk vomiting and then do the same, you have a greater sin because you saw a bad example and you imitated it.*

The same goes for when you imitate someone who is angry. He is like a drunken person, and his words are far worse than the vomit. And you are trying to imitate him!

And do not justify yourself by saying: "I did not start it," because even a killer could say: "I did not kill first." And this is exactly why you deserve a greater punishment because you were not able to hold yourself despite the fact that you saw the bad example".[32]

St Basil the Great: *"Normally, when you see him in this situation, you should be agitated and afraid not to be like him. By being angry is as if you said: "you did a good thing by being mad."*

But if anger is truly a bad thing, then why are you angry? Why don't you try to avoid being angry? And then you start insulting as well. Attack and counterattack with insults

---

[32] On Acts 31, 4 . P.G. 60, 232

After words, acts take place, led by the devil himself. After the first punches, the second punches back. Punches, kicks, scratches on both 'camps.' Their bodies are torn apart, but anger does not let them feel any pain.

This is why no matter how many wounds they might get, they do not calm down because all they care for is taking revenge on their brother. Most of the time, the one who gets angry and starts the fight takes disabilities or even death as trophies!" [33]

Has that evil battle resulted in you coming to your senses, at least? Have you hurried to the Christian images? Have you knelt down? Have you prayed in front of the crucified Lord in order to forgive you and your brother? If not, why don`t you do so?

---

[33] Against Anger 2. P.G. 31, 357

8. *"Do Not Let the Sun Go down"* [34]

"Be angry, and do not sin, do not let the sun go down on your wrath" (Eph. 4:26), says the Apostle Paul, and what he means is that in case you argue with your brother, you should reconcile as soon as possible.

St John Chrysostom: *"My dear, do not trap yourself, do not feel ashamed, or blushed and say: some moments ago we insulted each other, we said atrocious things and now how can we reconcile? By staying implacable, you give space to the devil, and you give a lot, actually! And the reconciliation will be more difficult. Because if a day passes, the shame will grow and it will become even bigger the second day. Same goes if you let three, four, five, ten, twenty, a hundred days go by. The wound will be incurable because as time goes by, we get further away from reconciliation".*

The Christian that quarreled with his brother (according to St John Chrysostom) has to do anything to meet him! Imagine how difficult it was back in the day without cars or mobile phones. He should wander for hours to find him. Can you imagine this? Our brother, wandering on foot

---

[34] St John Chrysostom, on statues , 20,5. P.G. 49, 205

through the whole city, going to every neighbor-hood, shop, square, church in order to reconcile with his brother! He writes:

"Run and catch your brother before he leaves. If it is necessary, go around or even outside the city, follow far distant routes, leave your work aside that day in order to be occupied by one thing: the reconciliation with your brother."

"If it seems exhausting, then think that it is for the sake of the Lord, and then you will find your strength. If your soul hesitates, blushes and feels shame, motivate it by saying times and times again: Why are you stalling? Why are you hesitating? This is not about money or any other mortal matter but about your salvation. That is what the Lord said to us, and everything else follows this. His commandments have the first place."

St John of the Ladder

"The beginning of meekness is the sealed lips while the soul is agitated.

The middle (of freedom) is when thoughts are in peace while the soul is a bit agitated.

And in the end, there should be tranquillity and peace in the sea of the soul despite the wild and impure winds." (Step 8th, 8).

Panagia

9. How Is Anger Controlled?

"He who is slow to anger is better than the mighty, and he who rules his spirit than he who takes a city" (Pr. 16:32)

"By the fear of the Lord one departs from evil" (Pr. 16:6). *"I have set the Lord always before me; Because He is at my right hand I shall not be moved"* (Ps. 16:8). *"My flesh trembles for fear of You"* (Ps. 119:120). The fear of God overcomes the "flesh"! It becomes an obstacle for sin. Joseph (son of the patriarch Jacob), by thinking that he was under God's surveillance, could control the passion of prostitution. *"How then can I do this great wickedness, and sin against God?"* (Gen. 39:9)

The fear of God can defeat the passion of anger too. *"The soldier in front of the king keeps his anger. The King is a human. If the presence of a human masters anger, let alone the presence of God!"*[35] The problem is we do not have this sense of the presence of God, and that is why we get angry. Thus, to overcome anger, we have to fight by

---

[35] St Basil the Great. Terms at length. Question 127. P.G. 31, 1168.

43

ourselves. And if we really try, we shall succeed (even without having the fear of God).

"I made haste, and did not delay to keep Your commandments" (Ps. 119:60). Let's suppose that we are trying to resolve an issue with our brother. If we keep in mind that we shall not react to anything he might do or say, we can already master anger. Or if we think that at that moment somebody is recording us with their phone, we will remain calm or even smile no matter how they insult us.

We wanted to, but we did not get angry. We brought anger under the control of reason, thus anger, just like a servant obeyed to the orders of its superior. That is what should happen. *"Anger should follow reason. Anger is the horse; reason is the bridle."* [36] And the horse obeys the orders of the bridle. In other words, the Christian fighter decides by himself how and when to get angry.

St John Chrysostom, in order to help the 'governor' make the passion obedient to reason, gives the following 'recipe': *"Imagine Lord's thorny chaplet, his gown, the wooden stick, the hits, the beatings, the spits, His humiliation. If we bear all*

---

[36] St, Basil the Great, Against Anger, 5 P. G.31, 365

these in mind, any rage we may have vanishes instantly." [37]

"*Says the Lord: "But on this one will I look: On him who is poor and of a contrite spirit, and who trembles at My word"* (Is. 66:2). The virtue of mildness is one important requirement for the Lord to show us His sympathy. Is there anything better than enjoying Lord's sympathy?

---

[37] Homily 84,3 on the Gospel of John P.G. 59, 458

"There's no better race under the sky than the Christians. Among the Christians, there's no better race than monks. However, what 'spoils' the commoners, as well as the monks, is hate and gossip. If they can throw them out of their lives, they will be able to live an angelic life on Earth." (Evergetinos, v.III. Case 2. Chapt. 8, 30).

PART II.
HATRED

1. Hatred Against Evil

Hatred is treated in the same way, as is anger. Just as anger has been given to us in order to use it against evil, hatred has been given to us in order to hate the evil (If we do not hate it, how can we be disjoined from it?).

St John of the Ladder saw three monks that had received insults.

The first bit his tongue got upset but did not speak.

The second was happy about himself because he was insulted and humiliated but felt sorry for those who insulted him.

The third wept with sorrow, thinking of his brothers' sin.[38]

The first, although he did not speak, the flame of passion ignited in him, and that is why he got upset. However, he fought and sealed his mouth.

---

[38] Step 8, on freedom from anger and on meekness, 28

Inside he might have had thoughts of hatred of his brothers, who knows?

The second behaved better than the first one. He did not get upset. He did not ignite any negative feelings towards his brothers. On the contrary, he felt happy for the insult and humiliation he received. He hated the insult (the sin) that his brothers committed, but he loved his brothers, and that is why he felt sorry for their terrible mistake.

The third behaved better than the second one. He did not even care for the benefit he received from the insults, he was not preoccupied with himself at all but only thought about his brothers. He hated the sin and loved the brothers.

So, the question is if we, lovers of the sin, can hate the sin and not the brother that commits it.

The answer is that as long as we sin, it is impossible to hate sin. In order to achieve our goal, we have to stop sinning in our mind by words or deeds. Otherwise, our hatred will always point towards our brother! So we had better stay far away from it.

Bitterness or Hatred?

I know an older woman whose husband was killed by a neighbor of hers when she was young during the 1960's. She has remained a widow ever since. Only by hearing the killer's name, she feels sick. Nevertheless, she says: *"I hope he's well! I don't want to see him suffer! I just can't stand seeing him!"*

Does this mean that she has feelings of hate inside her towards the murderer of her husband?

Of course not! She has been hurt in the soul and emotionally, and this wound (not the hate) makes her weak in the sight of her husband's murderer. A different thing could happen as well: hatred could be ignited in her, and as a consequence, she could curse him perpetually!

The Ladder of Divine Ascent

2. "The Devious Person"

"Woe to you, scribes and Pharisees, hypocrites! For you are like whitewashed tombs which indeed appear beautiful outwardly, but inside are full of dead men's bones and all uncleanness" (Mt. 23:27).

"Beware of the devious person," said our fathers because you never know what they may hide. Our fathers used to say this when they had to do with allegedly mild people who did not talk much. And they were right. It is possible that one day, these 'mild' people will get angrier than those who get more easily upset and will spill out the evilness they were holding back behind their 'mild' face!

Somebody gets heavily insulted. He gets angry and wants to counterattack, but he is not able to; he is afraid of the 'side-effects.' Out of necessity, he bears everything in silence; he 'swallows' them.[39] *"He just proved that he pretended to be a*

---

[39] Today he "swallows" this, the next day this, next day this, and so on, until his heart "freezes"! As a result, he gets alienated (psychologically) from that person, who may be his (or her) spouse! And the physical separation (alienation) results in bodily separation, divorce. In other words, di-

mild person. With his silence, he kept storing more hatred in him" [40] *"while he pretends to have love inside him. He is like a reef which is hidden underwater, hiding the danger."* [41]

Remember: Anger is the mirror of the soul. There is a moment when the quiet river becomes wild and spills out the evilness that it was keeping inside it the whole time. Like a sea full of waves that throws useless things on the surface and, in that way, cleans its bottom. Saint John of the Ladder says that: *"I saw people that ignited from the madness of the anger and they vomited their long-term kept evilness."* [42] They used one passion to get rid of the other.

Others keep holding hatred in their soul. *"They are more pathetic than the previous ones because they keep hatred inside them."*[43] The longer they keep it, the wilder it gets.

---

vorce does not come immediately, but it is prepared, for a long time in the souls.

[40] John of the Ladder. Step 8, on freedom from anger and on meekness, 18

[41] Abour Envy 6. P.G. 31, 385

[42] John of the Ladder. Ibid.

[43] Ibid

"Beware lest there be a wicked thought in your heart" (De. 15:9). Do not say anything nasty against your brother. Do not cast bad thoughts against the one who treats you badly. And if your thoughts beat you, try not to be beaten by these words. Do not speak badly behind his back because you are only going to increase your hatred. Close the 'tap.'

If you open your mouth: *"bless those who curse you, and pray for those who spitefully use you"* (Lk. 6:28). That is how you will find peace. Unless you are not really in favor of peace...!

St John the Evangelist

3. "Murderer"

St John the Evangelist[44] calls the Christian that hates his fellow human a murderer. *"Whoever hates his brother is a murderer, and you know that no murderer has eternal life abiding in him"* (1 Jn. 3:15).

St Nicodemus the Hagiorite explains:
"Christians that hate, mock and accuse their brothers resemble Cain, who murdered Abel. They are his imitators." [45] Possibly, we might ask what the correlation is between somebody who takes a knife and kills and somebody who just hates.

St Nicodemus answers: *"Those who hate their brothers might not have killed physically because they are not capable of such an act, but they kill their soul with their hatred every day. What did Esau do? He was killing his brother, Jacob, daily*

---

[44] *"My beloved children, love one another"*, it was his motto. Even when he was in his old age, and he was in bed, all he could do was to say it again and again *"my beloved children, love one another"*. Furthermore: Every Sunday when his spiritual children were "moving" him to the church, he would repeat the same *"love one another"* (Jn. 13: 34)

[45] St Nikodemos the Hagiorite. Explanation to the Seven Catholic Epistles. "Orthodox Kypseli" Thessaloniki, 1986, p. 535- 537

with his hatred and his enmity towards him. He hated Jacob because of the blessing that he received from their father: «let my father die, and after the days of mourn, I myself will kill Jacob.»" (Gen. 27:41)

St Nicodemus goes even further by saying that those who hate their brothers are far worse than those who kill physically.

First: *The murderer kills his fellow human being one time while he who hates him kills him daily either with accusations or slander.*

Second: *The murderer takes a human life while he who hates his brother kills his pride by presenting him as somebody with no pride and as a villain. This pride is greater than life; that is why many choose their pride over death.*

Third: *The murderer uses the sword against a mortal body, while the person who hates his brother uses it against his immortal soul".*

When he gets the chance, he does not hesitate to stab the sword into the heart of the other, killing him also physically, just as Herodias.[46]

Her hate for John the Baptist made her convince Herod to behead John the Baptist. Watch! She preferred to cut John's head, to having her daughter become the queen (and take half of Herod's kingdom). All because of hatred!

---

[46] John the Baptist "verified" Herod because he had "relationships" with Herodias, his brother's wife (Mk. 6:18). Thus, John became the most hated person for Herodias; *"for everyone practicing evil hates the light and does not come to the light, lest his deeds should be exposed"* (Jn. 3:20). *"He who corrects a scoffer gets shame for himself, and he who rebukes a wicked man only harms himself. Do not correct a scoffer, lest he hate you; Rebuke a wise man, and he will love you"* (Pr. 9:7-8).

The branch of the rose is thorny. However, we pay attention to the rose`s beauty rather than the thorns.

We hold it in our hand with caution and enjoy its beauty!

Why don't we do the same with our fellow humans?

Why do we keep staring at their thorns?

Is there a human that does not hide a diamond inside him?

4. Who Is the Loser? [47]

We have the illusion that by hating our brother, we somehow hurt him! We cannot possibly imagine that we only hurt ourselves. We are the losers! It is just to say that: *"hatred is a glass of poison that we drink instead of killing our enemy."*

When I do not like you, I suffer the consequences, not you. I cannot stand to see you while you might even want to see me. I stay up at night, torturing myself with sharp questions like: *"What did he do to me, this despicable person?"* While at the same time you could enjoy your sleep! My blood pressure is going up, not yours, and my nerves are broken, not yours, and there are many other similar questions that people, beaten by their passion, know well.

"Just like the madman (says St John Chrysostom), *the hater does not find peace because he keeps his enemy in mind all the time. If he hears his name, he becomes wild, feeling a great deal of pain. If he sees him in front of him, he shivers as if he was going through a great torture. Even if he sees a person close to his enemy, he will still get upset. Same goes for a personal belonging like a piece of*

---

[47] John Chrysostom, homily 20, 2 on statue. P.G.49, 200-1

59

clothing; he will still be upset! And we still think that by hating our enemy, we hurt him somehow! What a stupid thing!"

There is something worse: *"Just like a snake, it spills poison in your heart and eats you from the inside. It devours little by little the will of the soul for virtue, and as a result, you live for the sin without having any energy left for the virtue."* [48]

There is something even worse! If we do not forgive our fellow humans cordially, the Lord is not going to forgive our sins! And again, St John (Chrysostom) says to us: *"Is there a worse thing than hatred when that becomes an obstacle deviating us from the grace of God and the forgiveness of our sins?"* He continues:

"When you hate, you hate at the expense of yourself and not anybody else's because it is your sins that are not forgiven, not the sins of the other. Whatever malevolence you do against your enemy is valid as long as he is alive. But your punishment is the eternal hell! Whatever you do to yourself cannot be compared to what your fellow human being does to you! Do not stab the sword in your heart then!" [49]

---

[48] Symeon the New Theologian. 154 practical & theological chapters. Philokalia v.IV.
[49] Honily 61, 4, 5 on the Gospel of Matthew, P.G. 58, 594

"You want to be a hater? Hate the devil. Stab him instead. And stab him to the bone!" [50]

---

[50] Homily 14, 2 to Ephesians P.G. 62, 102.

St King David

5. The 'Eye' of a Hater

"Is this your voice, my son David?" (1 Sam. 24:16) said Saul to David at the end of his adventure. But it was not the first time that Saul heard David's voice! What happened?

St John Chrysostom explains: *"Just as the clouds cover the beauty of the sky making him look black instead of blue so does hatred cover somebody's face making him look different. When the clouds disperse, you can see the sky's beauty. In the same way, when hatred disperses, we can see the other person as he is, just like in the case of Saul. His hatred (like clouds) could not let him hear David's voice. It seemed disturbing, repulsing. Now that the passion has gone, he could hear him just fine, and he was able to recognize David's voice!"* [51]

To a glass of clear water, you add a drop of ink. The clear water becomes inky, it blackens. The eye of the hater works the same way. He spills out ink a *"vomit of passions"* (poison), he aims at the other person's face, and he smears it. And in this 'smeary' situation presents it, in order to humiliate him socially. (Homicide!)

---

[51] Homily 3rd, 5 on David & Saul. P.G. 54,702

"I drive carefully, and I don't exceed speed lim-its," bragged a driver. Next to him, another driver was driving at the same speed. Do you know what he said to him? *"He's slower than a turtle"!* He did not even know the man. Imagine what he could have said if he had known him and even hated him! *"A common characteristic of the envious and the haters is: to accuse and distort the disciplines and the virtues of the other person, beaten by and full of the horrible spirit of hate."* [52]

Let's suppose that you hate your co-worker. You do not want to see or hear him. If, by chance, you meet him in a company, you do not look at him like everybody else, your look changes. Whatever he says or does you blacken it or smear it. *"Look the way he's sitting!"* (although he is sitting normally) *"Look how he's staring!"* (although he is looking normally), *"look how he's talking"* (although he is talking normally). *"Did you hear what he said?"* People around you cannot see any of these things. They see a different person! [53]

---

[52] John of the Ladder. Step 10th on slander, 13
[53] What accusation these people would tell us for their brothers which hate them, will hear them as holy Gospel! So we also have a problem ...!

St Basil the Great: *"The crows may fly over valleys, flowers, beautiful landscapes, but they are not enchanted by them, and they rather run towards dead bodies. That is what haters do, as well. They prefer staring at the other person's weaknesses! They do not pay attention to the great things that the other has achieved."*

"Without any difficulty, they call the other person's virtues evil. They call the courageous person audacious, the wise, insensible, the just, rough, the frugal, stingy! And that is because their soul is deep in passion so they cannot see clearly. They cannot see virtue, only evil." [54]

An obvious example is that of high priests, scribes, and Pharisees. They ended up saying that Christ gets rid of the demons with the power of Beelzebub (Lucifer). Hearing Him preaching at the temple, they took stones to throw at Him, and they were in a temple. They told Him that he was a Samaritan (the worst thing for a Jew) and that the devil was working through Him and many more similar things!

---

[54] About envy 5, P. G. 31, 381-2

"Snakes and beasts fight with those who disturb them because they act out of instinct. However, people have a reason not only not to repulse those who make them sad but even to be able to love those who hate them. Due to our egoism, we can love neither those who hate nor those who love us! Thus, our behavior is worse than the beasts and the snakes!" (St Maximus the Confessor, Ascetical logos 8, 367).

"Where are those who wonder why beasts are so wild? Why are scorpions venomous? Why do vipers have such strong venom? Look! Man has a worse sense of hatred than the beasts! Not by nature like the beasts but by choice" (St John Chrysostom, Homily on Psalm 139. P.G. 55, 419).

6. *"You Take No Notice?"*

"If you're not in good terms with your fellow human, then you are not in good terms with God."
Jews were stepping over the weak (Is. 58:4). At the same time, they were fasting. They were saying to the Lord: *"Why have we fasted, 'they say' and You have not seen?"* (Is. 58:3) (at that time fasting was equal to a total food abstention). The Lord replied: *"In fact, in the day of your fasting, you find pleasure, and exploit all your laborers"* (Is. 58:3). He would only "notice" them if they could change their lifestyle! (Is. 58:6-8). *"Then you shall call, and the Lord will answer; you shall cry, and He will say, 'Here I am'"* (Is. 58:9). In other words, before you end your prayer because of your change, He will reply: *"Here I am!"* with big joy.

And if this is true for the Old Testament, imagine the New. *"Therefore if you bring your gift to the altar, and there you remember that your brother has something against you, leave your gift there before the altar, and go your way. First be reconciled to your brother, and then come and offer your gift"* (Mt. 5:23-24).
At that time, Israel had only one temple in Jerusalem. It is possible that someone started from Capernaum to offer his present. When he reached

the temple, he remembered that there was an argument between him and his brother in Capernaum. He was obliged to leave the present at the place of sacrifices, go back to Capernaum, find his brother, make peace with him, and then return to Jerusalem to offer his present.

If that is how the Lord reacts when somebody else has something against you, imagine how He would react if you had something against somebody else!

He does not accept your prayer or your gift, neither a hardcore fasting nor even your terrible torture. Take the case of the priest Saprikios as an example. He was suffering for Christ, and at the same time, he hated his brother Nikiforos. Thus, the grace of God, which led him to martyrdom, abandoned him, and he denied Christ. All because of hatred! [55]

---

[55] The Great Synaxaristis of Orthodox Church, v. 2nd, edition 5th Athens 1985, p. 248-259

7. The Way to Hell

"Whoever hates his brother is a murderer, and you know that no murderer has eternal life abiding in him" (1 Jn. 3:15). In other words, he is damned to hell. And justly! How can he take part in the kingdom of God, which is the kingdom of love? In the life of St Dionysius the Areopagite we read:

One time, he went to Crete and stayed at the house of a priest under the name Karpos. This priest did not like an idolater because he was trying to influence a Christian. The priest was praying to God to take both of them with Him because they were endangering his flock. And something extraordinary happened as Saint Dionysius narrates.

As he was praying, his house began to shake from the ground; his roof opened wide. He saw Christ sitting on a throne surrounded by angels! Fire was falling from the sky to the ground! The house's floor was cut open in two, forming a huge, dark canyon! At the edge of the canyon, the two idolaters were standing astonished. From the depths of the canyon, snakes were thrown to the surface, and they were hissing to them and hitting them with their tails in order to throw them into the canyon and die!

The priest took pity on the two idolaters who were still standing there. He lifted his head and looked towards the sky; He saw Christ standing up from His throne and moving towards the end of the edge with His angels in an effort to save the idolaters! He approached the priest and said to him: *"I'm ready to suffer a thousand times for the savior of all mankind! And you don't feel sorry for the loss of your brothers!"* and He added: *"Be careful! You might end up in hell because of your hatred!"*[56]

Not only thieves, cheaters, dishonest people, defectors go to hell but also "murderers" that have hatred and evilness in their hearts!

---

[56] The Great Synaxaristis of Orthodox Church, v. 10, edition 5th Athens 1983, p. 68-69

Apostle Paul

"Now the works of the flesh are evident, which are: ... sorcery, hatred, contentions, jealousies, outbursts of wrath, selfish ambitions, dissensions, heresies, envy... and the like; of which I tell you beforehand, just as I also told you in time past, that those who practice such things will not inherit the kingdom of God" (Gal. 5:19-20).

St John the Evangelist

8. Hatred and Holy Communion

"If someone says "I love God" and hates his brother, he is a liar; for he who does not love his brother whom he has seen, how can he love God whom he has not seen?" (1 Jn. 4:20). *"He who does not love his brother abides in death"* (1 Jn. 3:14) away from Christ, who is Resurrection and Life. (Jn. 11:25) How can such a man receive the Holy Communion, unite with Christ, and at the same time, be away from Him?

Reminder: Lord said that if you get your present to the temple, and there you remember that your brother has something against you, leave the present, go find your brother, make peace with him and then offer Him your present. (Mt. 5:23-24). Remember how cleansed you have to be in front of Him in order to receive communion. *"Man, now that you intend to commune with the Body of the Lord, firstly reconcile with everyone that has done you wrong."* [57]

Thus, the first thing you have to do before receiving communion is to "make up" with your brother, who made you sad. Who before receiving communion seeks for his brother? We receive

---

[57] Holy Communion Service

communion and transgress the Lord's com-mandment! [58]

St John Chrysostom would say to his spiritual children: *"I warn you! I rebel and shout as loud as I can! No one from those who have hatred in them can go near the Mysteries. Do you have an enemy? Do not receive Holy Communion! Do you want to receive Holy Communion? Make peace, and then come!"* [59]

And St John comparing the hater to the pros-titute, the hater is worse than the prostitute! *"He who prostitutes is not allowed to go near the holy mysteries. Same goes for who has an enemy and hates, even more for him because the prostitute sins occasionally while the hater sins perpetually."* [60]

---

[58] Our grandparents, before to receive the Holy Commun-ion, were running from neighborhood to neighborhood, asking for forgiveness, regardless of whether they were guilty or not! They also were fasting for one week, and in the last three days without oil! Today, with the same ease that we receive the "antidote" we receive the Holy Body and the Blood of the Lord!

[59] Homily 20,5 on statue P.G. 49, 204

[60] Homily 20,1 on statue P.G. 49, 198

And what happens if he receives the Holy Communion without making peace? He does not receive communion from Christ but the devil! [61]

---

[61] The easiest way for the devil to possess a Christian is where the Christian is unworthy of partaking Holy Communion. *"He immediately possesses those that have un-worthily participated in Holy Communion!"* (St John Chrysostom. Homily on the betrayal of Judas I, P.G: 49: 380). He possessed Judas with such ease! *"And then* (when he had taken Holy Communion!) *Satan entered him"* (Jn. 13:27).

The Ladder of Divine Ascent

9. How Is Hatred Beaten?

St John of the Ladder says that love is an easy thing because love is innate. (Hate is unnatural; a sickness!). *"Let be ashamed those who say that they cannot love."* [62]

St John Chrysostom agrees with him. He says:

"Is there an easier thing than to stop feeling anger and rage against the person who was unfair toward us? Is this about a long trip? Give money? Beg others? [63] *Fast while we cannot due to sickness? Of course not! And here is God's charity. In order to follow the most important commandments that embellish our lives, no physical effort is required.*[64] *What is required is just the will.*[65]

If the King created a new law obliging enemies to become friends; otherwise, everybody would be beheaded, how would we react? Wouldn't we rush to make peace? We listen to the king, who is a fellow human servant but not to God. Thus, do we deserve forgiveness?" [66]

---

[62] Step 26, on discernment of thoughts 41
[63] Homily 20,3 on statue P.G. 49, 201
[64] Homily 20,1 on statue P.G. 49, 198
[65] Homily 20,3 on statue P.G. 49, 201
[66] Homily 20,5 on statue P.G. 49, 206

Medicaments

St John Chrysostom: *"Whoever talks about their enemy does not even refer to him by using his name but use 'nicknames' instead, like the horrible, crazy, weird person, etc. However, you, my dear, when you refer to your enemy, use his name and talk about him with respect. When your soul listens to these words, it will slowly comply with your mouth, and then it will make peace with your enemy. Good words are the best medicament for the cure of the soul."* [67]

"Bless those who curse you" (Mt. 5:44) *"Being reviled; we bless; being persecuted, we endure; being defamed, we entreat. We have been made as the filth of the world"* (1 Cor. 4:12-13), said Paul. Praying is the same cure (and in a greater scale) for our soul. *"Pray for those who spitefully use you and persecute you"* (Mt. 5:44).

Again: *"Where is the difficulty in praying for our enemy? Do we have to pay taxes or dig pits all day? The hatred in us is the difficulty. Nevertheless, how can we beat it if we do not try?"* *"Let's fight in order not to hate anyone and in order to be loved*

---

[67] Homily 1st, 6 on David & Saul. P.G. 54, 686

by God! And even if we have obligations towards Him, He will show His mercy." [68]

---

[68] John Chrysostom, homily 61st, 4 on the Gospel of the Matthew. P.G. 58, 596

"Let nothing be done through selfish ambition or conceit, but in lowliness of mind, let each esteem others better than himself. Let each of you look out not only for his own interests, but also for the interests of others" (Phil. 2:3-4).

"Let each of us please his neighbor for his good, leading to edification" (Rom. 15:2)

"Do not be overcome by evil, but overcome evil with good" (Rom. 12:21).

10. The Innocent Makes the First Move

Christ says: *"...if your brother sins against you, go and tell him his fault between you and him alone. If he hears you, you have gained your brother"* (Mt. 18:15).

You see that Christ addresses the innocent to meet the guilty, *"because the guilty is not in place to confront the innocent."* [69] It is similar to this: *"if you bring your gift to the altar, and there remember that your brother has something against you, leave your gift there before the altar, and go your way. First be reconciled to your brother, and then come and offer your gift"* (Mt. 5:23-24).

"Can you imagine? (St John Chrysostom wonders and admires). *The Lord accepts that you leave aside your present for Him! He does not consider it as a shameful act. And you think it is shameful to go first and make peace with your brother? Is that something to forgive? Do not wait for him to come to you first. You should run if you want to get the trophy.[70] Whoever runs first gets the trophy!"* [71] *"God begs us every day, and we do*

---

[69] Homily 60, 1 ,on the Gospel of Matthew P.G. 58, 584
[70] Homily 20, 5 on statues P.G. 49, 204
[71] Homily 20, 3 on statues P.G. 49, 202

not pay attention to Him, and despite knowing that, He keeps begging us, you are not able to beg your fellow human servant? How can you be saved?" [72]

When they were saying to St John (Chrysostom) that *"If I speak he will become worse,"* he replied: *"He will become worse if you do not make peace with him. No matter how tough he is when he sees you approaching him, he will appreciate it".* [73] To those who were saying: *"If I went first it would be as if I was guilty and he was innocent,"* he would reply: *"Excuses! All this is just to cover your evil thoughts. God can see your hearts and your motivation."* [74]

"Man! If you wait for the other person to talk to you first you have done nothing important! On the contrary you have been spiritually downgraded. If you approach him first God will compliment you! What is better than this? What is more ridiculous than waiting for the other person to come and find you? What is worse than this insensibility? How vain is this? What pride is this?" [75]

---

[72] Homily 20, 6 on statues P.G. 49, 207
[73] Homily 20, 4 on statues P.G. 49, 204
[74] Homily 20, 4 on statues P.G. 49, 204
[75] Homily 3rd, 3 on David and Saul P.G.54, 698

"Christ sacrificed himself in order for you to be reconciled with God and you do not even accept to say a word first!" [76] *"How do you expect the Lord to be mild to you when you are tough towards your fellow human being by refusing to forgive him?"* [77]

"Don't we deserve hell when we beg others, spend money, flatter in order for us to win earthly things?" [78] *"But when it comes to obeying God's laws, we do not want to beg our brother who made us sad, but we think that it is a shame? Tell me, why are you feeling ashamed when you are going to win something out of it? It is a shame when you keep your passion inside you."* [79]

---

[76] Homily 20, 5 on statues P.G. 49, 204
[77] Homily 20, 1 on statues P.G. 49, 198
[78] Homily 20, 3 on statues P.G. 49, 201
[79] Homily 20, 3 on statues P.G. 49, 202

Icon of Christ

11. *"If Your Enemy Is Hungry"*
(Rom. 12:20)

Jesus Christ: *"I say to you, love your enemies, bless those who curse you do good to those who hate you and pray for those who spitefully use you and persecute you"* (Mt. 5:44). As we see, Christ does not only want us not to hate our enemy, pray for him, or not accuse him, He also wants us to love him and be his benefactor! *"Nothing can be compared to loving our enemies and benefiting those who treat us badly."*[80]

"If your enemy is hungry, feed him; if he is thirsty, give him a drink; for in so doing you will heap coals of fire on his head." (Rom. 12:20). But that way, it would be as if you were seeking revenge! Again St John (Chrysostom) explains it to us:

"This part gave to many the reason to blame Paul. From one hand he teaches indulgence and philanthropy and from the other hand he encourages us to set fire on our enemy's head". The saint explains: *"Undoubtedly, giving your enemy food and water is great. But, by saying that with this act*

---

[80] John Chrysostom homily 84,3 on the Gospel of John. P.G. 59, 458

you set fire on his head he makes us having doubts. You show mercy but at the same time, you give yourself a greater punishment. But Paul meant something else".

"He knew well how difficult it is to reconcile quickly with the enemy. Not by nature but by our character. In order to make it easy he used a bait: «you set fire on your enemy's head» when you benefit him! By giving this glimpse of revenge you rush to benefit him. It is a win-win situation.

You: slowly throw away the desire for punishment and you become his friend. Nobody would accept to have the person that feeds as an enemy even if initially, he had other intentions.

Your enemy: he will become your friend. He would not be so horrible and insensible not to make the person his friend who feeds him![81]

We should not give up the fight until our enemy loves us. It is not enough just not to despise him, or not to mistreat him, but we should try to remove hatred from his heart and make him feel comfortable and pleasant with us." [82]

"If he does not want to be reconciled with us he will be the great loser. God will not forgive him.

[81] Homily if your enemy is hungry 5. P.G. 51, 180-184.
[82] Homily 20, 6 on statue. P.G. 49, 207

You on the other side will be rewarded for your effort.[83]

Christ prayed for his crucifiers (Lk. 23:34), but because they did not show repentance, they were slaughtered. *"Do not pray for these people, nor lift up a cry or prayer for them, nor make intercession to Me,"* said the Lord to the prophet Jeremiah *"for I will not hear you!"* (Jer. 7:16) because they would not repent.

St John Chrysostom

12. What Is Your Gain?

St John Chrysostom: *"You will say: I begged my enemy many times in order to reconcile, but he was negative. Because you begged many times your reward is going to be great, same as his punishment"* [84] (God judges everything!).

"We committed great sins in front of God. We made him mad! But his philanthropy has showed us the means in order to calm him down: The reconciliation with our brother. How do we deserve His forgiveness if we fail in it?" [85]

"Do not say that your brother insulted you, defamed you, did wrong to you. Because the more wrong he did to you, the more things you win. First and foremost, you are getting cleansed from your sins. Then you acquire forbearance and patience; you become indulgent and a philanthropist. Do you know what is the greatest of all? You acquire the philanthropy of the Lord, gaining boldness. Let's fight then in order not to hate anyone if we want to be loved by God, and if in the end, we are indebted in front of Him, He will have mercy on us. When we love our enemies, we benefit ourselves".[86]

---

[84] Homily 20, 6 P.G. 49, 207
[85] Homily 20, 5. P.G. 49, 206
[86] Homily 61, 4 on the Gospel of Matthew. P.G. 58, 594-596

The Pacemakers

"Blessed are the peacemakers, For they shall be called sons of God" (Mt. 5:9) because the son of God came to earth in order to unite the 'gaps' and reconcile those who have hatred among them. *"You see, the Lord does not ask from His servants just to get rid of their disputes, their hatred but something more: make the other reconcile as well!"* [87]

Let's say that two brothers have argued badly. The first threatens the second that he will kill him. The situation is crucial. At the last moment, you reconcile them. Thanks to your intervention, no brotherly blood was spilled! As a peacemaker, you will be called a 'son of God' (Mt. 5:9). And only from this, you shall receive a great reward!

We will be surprised in the afterlife!

---

[87] Homily 15, 4 on the Gospel of Matthew. P.G.57,228

13. The Devil and Reconciliation

If the one who tries to reconcile with his fellow-men is called by Christ 'son of God' (Mt. 5:9), the one who separates them is definitely 'son of the devil.'

Devil, comes from the Greek verb 'διαβάλλω' which means to make someone a rival, an enemy. That is what the devil does. He separates us (with his hatred). He is happy to see people fighting. He despises reconciliation!

Two monks were in the desert. They loved each other. The devil was trying to separate them. One night the younger did some damage. He overturned the lamp, and they stayed in the dark. The other one got angry and hit him. The 'guilty' one humiliated himself and asked for forgiveness.

Immediately after this, the devil's power was shattered. Incapable of teasing the brothers, he left them alone. He went to his superior to report, that was sitting in a temple of idols. He reported to him what had happened. At the temple, there was the priest of idols as well. He was so shaken that he decided to be baptized and to become a monk. As a monk, he was spreading the word: I have heard the devil saying: *"When I make these two monks fight, and one of them asks for for-giveness, my power disappears!"* [88]

The same happens everywhere, at the family as well. If the spouse's fight and the guilty one asks for forgiveness, the devil leaves the house. But *"whoever stays cold with each other they give place to the devil,"*[89] i.e., they have the devil as their 'housemate'!

---

[88] Evergetinos v. 1. Case 45, 62
[89] John Chrysostom, Homily 20,5 on statue P.G. 49, 205

14. Hatred in the Old Testament

Christ said to Jews: *"You have heard that it was said: You shall love your neighbor and hate your enemy. But I say to you, love your enemies"* (Mt. 5: 43-44).

The enemy for the Jew, who believed in the true God, was the idolater who believed in fake gods. So, everyone who believed in the true God was considered a brother. And Jews were obliged to love everyone who believed in the true God (their compatriot and every stranger who had the same belief).

Lord was saying to them: *"... nor shall you take a stand against the life of your neighbor"* (Lev. 19:16). *"You shall not hate your brother in your heart"* (Lev. 19:17). *"You shall not take vengeance, nor bear any grudge against the children of your people, but you shall love your neighbor as yourself: I am the Lord."* (Lev. 19:18). *"Execute true justice, Show mercy and compassion to one another do not oppress the widow or the fatherless, the alien or the poor. Let none of you plan evil in his heart against his brother"* (Zech. 7:8-10).

On the contrary, everyone who did not believe in true God but in idols was considered as an enemy by Jews, and they were obligated to hate them. Some examples:

A woman of Canaan (an idolater) approached the Lord. She was talking to Him, but since he was Jewish did not reply to her! (Mt. 15:23). He called idolaters 'dogs' (Mt. 15:26)!

It was prohibited for an idolater to be buried in the same graveyard with a Jewish. (Mt. 27:7)

If a Jew had relations with an idolater around Passover, he was considered 'dirty.' It was prohibited for him to sit at the Passover table. (Num. 9:6-11). High priests and Pharisees, when they took Jesus to the idolater Pilatus ", *they themselves did not go into the Praetorium, lest they should be defiled, but that they might eat the Passover*" (Jn. 18:28).

This commandment was in power in the Old Testament. But wasn't it a sin to hate their enemy? As the commandment was God's, it was not a sin. It would have been a sin if they had loved their enemy. And why hate him?

In order for a Jew not to have any relation with an idolater, God dictated that he was his enemy, and he should avoid him. So, an idolater was considered as someone 'dirty' by Jews.

And now they can hear this from Christ that they have to love and benefit their enemies! "*I say to you, love your enemies, bless those who curse you, do good to those who hate you, and pray for those who spitefully use you and persecute you"* (Mt. 5:44). It was the first time that these words were heard in the world.

If, as Christians, we love those who love us, in what way are we different from the thieves, the prostitutes, the terrorists who love each other?

"But if you love those who love you, what credit is that to you? For even sinners love those who love them. And if you do good to those who do good to you, what credit is that to you? For even sinners do the same" (Lk. 6:32-33)

15. Hate Among Christians

If the Lord wanted the Jews to stay united, be-loved imagine how much He demands from us Christians. He said to His (Jewish) disciples: *"A new commandment I give to you, that you love one another; as I have loved you, that you also love one another."* (Jn. 13:34). A little before His Crucifix-ion, He said a special prayer. He told God, His fa-ther: *"I do not pray for these alone, but also for those who will believe in Me through their word; that they all may be one, as You, Father, are in Me, and I in You; that they also may be one in Us"* (Jn. 17:20-21).

He added: *"that the world may believe that You sent Me"* (Jn. 17:21). This means that the most significant motive for the faithless is not miracles but the love among Christians!. When they see churchmen and commoners united in love! This love works more efficiently in the con-sciousness of the faithless than a miracle! *"By this all will know that you are My disciples, if you have love for one another"* (Jn. 13:35), Jesus said once again!

Thus, hatred, disputes among priests, and, most particularly, high priests, public debated is the worst thing possible for our church. It divides the church without mercy, and it upsets the flock.[90] The worst thing is: it 'sticks' the faithless to their unfaithfulness and the heretics to their heresy. That is why St Basil (the Great) considered disputes among priests as something *"horrendous!"* [91]

When he learned that the clergy of Samosata were fighting with each other, he felt deep sorrow in his heart, as he wrote to them.[92] He also wrote that he wanted to go and meet these priests personally, and to advise them himself, but he was not in the place to do so! He was ill, and trips were long and tiring! That is why, without wasting a minute, he sent an urgent letter begging them to reconcile. And when they do so, to let him know that they stopped arguing.[93]

It is a bad thing to have excrements in front of one's door.

It is even worse to see them and not to do anything about them.

What is worse than this is to add some more.

What is worse than this is to have such a thing in front of a church.

---

[90] Basil the Great, about God's Judgment 1 P.G. 31,633
[91] Epistle 219 to the Clergy of Samosata 1..G. 32, 812
[92] Ibid
[93] Ibid

It is even worse to be able to clean them up
and not to do anything about them.

St Symeon the New Theologian

PART III.
ENVY

1. Hatred and Envy

"*By nature, one can find jealousy in us for virtues, and we tend to turn this into something evil.*"[94] In other words, it is natural to feel jealous of the good thing of somebody else, his house he bought or made, the progress of his son, etc. That is not to be blamed or considered as a sin. However, if we do not pay attention to this natural, innate characteristic, it can be turned to envy. Thus, we will not only be jealous but also hate him for having something good. Envy means to be jealous and hate the other person!

If the hater is prohibited from Holy Communion, it is even more true for the one who envies his brother!

If the eye of the hater distorts the virtues of the other, he sees them as flaws, the eye of the envious person does even greater damage.

---

[94] John of the Ladder, Step 26, on discernment of thoughts, passions and virtues, B,41

If it is true, *"whoever hates his brother is a murderer"* (1 Jn. 3:15), then it is even more true for the one who envies his brother!

If it is true, *"he who does not love his brother abides in death"* (1 Jn. 3:14). It is true for the one who envies his brother.

If hatred *"spills poison to one's heart, eating you up from inside,"* [95] think how much poison the snake of envy spills!

If the hater does not have a place in God's Kingdom (but rather in hell together with the demons), let alone the envious person!

What can an envious person do in Paradise? See the glories of his friend, his brother, and then collapse because of envy? At least, in Hell, he will see his people being tortured, and he will be relieved. He is 'inappropriate' for Paradise and 'appropriate' for Hell.

---

[95] Symeon the New Theologian. 154 practical 7 theological chapters, 31. Philokalia v. 4th.

2. Envy, Vanity

"Let us not become conceited, provoking one another, envying one another" (Gal. 5:26).

Vanity means empty, earthly glory. *"Observe, and you will realize that the vain man stays alive even in the tomb! He thinks about the perfumes and ornaments that he will have at his funeral."* [96] Imagine the extent of his sickness!

Vanity appears mainly in the chase of prestige because these are followed by glory and admiration. For example, what makes the vain person (and who is not one?) eager to achieve the rank of the high priest? It is not his willingness to offer help to the church but the prestige that accompanies it!

If he wants to serve the church, he will have to do it without any ranks. Just think about it: if the rank of the high priest was not accompanied by fanfares, glory, and prestige, but only worries and disputes who would accept it? If the high priest was as simple as a priest without welcoming receptions, fanfares, without bows, golden sticks, or thrones who would crave for it? If all of the activity was limited to an office, to write or

---

[96] John of the Ladder. Step 21, on vanity, 4

read or sign papers and then to go to his cell who would go after such a 'dull' rank? Who?

"Let us not become conceited, provoking one another, envying one another" (Gal. 5:26), said Paul, meaning that the passion of vanity creates envy: *"It is from vanity that comes envy."* [97] We can see that clearly from the Pharisees.

"All their works they do to be seen by men" (Mt. 23:5). *"They do a charitable deed in the synagogues and in the streets, that they may have glory from men"* (Mt. 6:2). *"They love to pray standing in the synagogues and on the corners of the streets, that they may be seen by men"* (Mt.6: 5). They fast, *"and they disfigure their faces that they may appear to men to be fasting"* (Mt. 6:16). Vanity runs through their veins!

So, when they saw Christ 'stealing' their glory, they envied Him. Their vanity led them to envy. The first passion led to another.

And by the way: *"there is an interconnection between commandments. When a commandment is transgressed, then, by consequence, others will follow".* [98] Vanity brings envy, envy brings hate,

---

[97] John Chrysostom, homily 5th, 6 to Galatians. P.G. 61,674
[98] Basil the Great, Terms at length 1, 2 P.G. 31, 893

hate brings murder, etc. *"whoever shall keep the whole law, and yet stumble in one point, he is guilty of all"* (James 2:10).

Something similar happens with virtues; the first leads to the next. E.g. *"when you behave with mildness towards your enemy, you acquire indulgence, patience, grace in front of the eyes of the Lord."* [99]

---

[99] John Chrysostom, Homily 61, 4 on the Gospel of Matthew, P.G. 58, 594

Cain Killing Abel

3. The Sickness of Affinity

King Solomon said: *"I saw that for all toil and every skillful work a man is envied by his neighbor"* (Eccl. 4:4). In other words: why do you own such a good car and I do not? I may be poor, but I will work hard in order to buy one myself and even better than yours so that you become jealous of me. *"This also is vanity and grasping for the wind"* (Eccl. 4:4).

St Basil (the Great): *"Envy manifests against our relatives. A person from Skiathos will not be the envy of an Egyptian but of a fellow citizen; and not any fellow citizen but his neighbor; and not any neighbor but the one that has the same profession as him; and not any relative but his brother. Just like fire produces smoke, envy is being produced among friends and relatives. Envy is the sickness of friendship and affinity"*.[100]

You learn that an immigrant, a stranger to you, wins 5,000,000 dollars in the lottery. You are not going to envy him! But, if you learn that this lucky person is your friend, your cousin, you will envy him! You will stay up all night because of it!

---

[100] About Envy 4. P.G. 31, 380.

Cain envied his brother Abel. (Gen. 4:5). Jacob's children envied their brother Joseph. (Gen. 37:20). Eusebius of Caesarea envied the Saint and Great Basil. Because of this, Basil was obliged to flee from Cappadocia during a difficult time for the church![101] He was also envied by his uncle, his mother's brother, Bishop Gregory! Because his nephew (Basil) became Archbishop! He refused any contact with him! The gap was bridged with the intervention of Saint Basil's brother, Saint Gregory, Bishop of Nyssa![102]

The microbe of envy is so powerful that it can strike anybody. Even Saints! It has been wisely said: *"when you hear an Elder to glorify his neighbor* (Elder) *more than himself, he is at a very high spiritual level!"* [103]

Let's not have the illusion that the microbe of envy cannot affect us, as if we had immunity!

"Let's avoid such an unbearable evil. It is diabolical, a marriage with hell, an obstacle to re-

---

[101] Stylianos Papadopoulos. Professor of the University of Athens. The life of a Great. Basil of Caeisaria. "Apostoliki Diakonia". Athens, p. 196-200
[102] Ibid p. 292-298
[103] Gerontikon. Abba Matoe, 7.

*spect, a path to hell, deprivation of the Heavenly
Kingdom."* [104]

---

[104] Basil the Great, about envy 5. P.G. 31, 380

St Basil The Great

4. Torture

"Just like rust destroys iron, so does envy your soul. You keep inside a harrowing torture that cannot be released. There is nothing to say or admit. How can you say that you are sad because of your brother's happiness?" [105]

Once, they said to an envious man: *"If I do something good to you, I will do it twice to your brother. If you get a thousand dollars, I will give him two thousand. What do you want me to do for you?"* And he replied: *"take out my eye so that you can take out both of his eyes!"* The only thing that gives him any satisfaction is your misery!

Indeed, *"envy is the most abhorrent passion that grows in peoples' souls! He wishes to see bad things happen to the other, in order to feel relief! To become pitiable from laudable. He calms down and becomes his friend when he sees him crying or mourning, pretending that he feels pity for him. He reminds him of his previous situation not out of philanthropy but out of cold-heartedness, in order to hurt him even more. He glorifies wealth when the other person does not have it in order to make him suffer even more. He glorifies beauty and health when the other person is sick and withered.*

---

[105] Basil the Great, About Envy 2. P.G. 31, 373,

111

He glorifies (after death) the kid, "how beautiful and smart he was," but while he was alive, he would not have said a single thing!" [106]

The same happens everywhere, even in the Church. Priests do not say anything good about their fellow who works with dedication and modesty for the salvation of people! They can even comment on (with malevolence) some minor flaws instead of the other person's virtues. When he dies, they glorify him. *"He was great!" "a saint!" "he was..."* while before, they did not even want to hear anything about him!"

"It is possible for the envious person to do something else: when he sees the others glorifying the dead, he cannot stand it! He is trying to change their opinion because of envying even the dead!" [107] Insane things from sane (?) people!

---

[106] Ibid p. 373, 376
[107] Ibid

5. Envy and Murder

If hatred brings murder, envy is even worse. The envious person is more dangerous than the hater.

When the envious person sees that the other is in a good place, he feels torture and seeks some kind of medicine in order to find relief. The only solution is to see the other person suffering. But in order to suffer, he has to hurt him; torture him. Examples:

Saul, the king, was after the little and thin David with his troops chasing him in the mountains and valleys in order to kill him! All that out of envy! (1. Sam. 22. 23. 24).

Cain was also suffering from envy, so he decided to murder his brother Abel in cold blood. (Gen. 4:8)

Jacob's children envied their brother Joseph and decided to kill him. And they would have done it if it had not been for Reuben. What did they do? (Gen. 37:20). They throw him in a pit, without having any regrets. We do not know how big this pit was, but it must have been deep. Joseph began to cry in the dark while his brothers were having dinner. In order to get rid of him, they sold him as a slave to the Ishmaelites that

113

happened to be around. (Gen. 37:24-28). Out of envy!

The religious leaders of Israel, high priests, scribes, Pharisees, put aside their spiritual mission, and they were occupied with the persecution of Christ. During three years of his public life, they were not doing anything but planning how to kill Jesus! Their envy led them to murder. *"For he* (Pilatus) *knew that they had handed Him over because of envy"* (Mt. 27:18).

Above all, we have the "father" of envy, i.e., the devil! He could not stand seeing Adam and Eve enjoying Paradise, which he has lost out of envy! And he did everything to ruin their happiness. He deceived them and threw them out, not from Hell but Paradise![108] *"Through the devil's envy, he* (man) *was deceived and partook of the food*

---

[108] He created a 'satanic' plan. He read the mind of Adam and Eve. And he decided to approach Eve at the moment she was alone. He did not tell her the reason why he was approaching her, because she would have asked for protection from Adam. He spoke to her tenderly, fatherly, until he succeeded! (Gen. 3:1-6). And he went away. That is what he does! Once he kills his victim, he runs for other cases! *"When a man is captivated by all his passions, the devil leaves him, because the 'work' that the devil would do is done by the passions!"* (St John of the Ladder. Step 26, On Discernment of Thoughts, Passions and Virtues, 40).

and became a transgressor of your command-ments; Lord, he again returns condemned to the earth from whence he came."[109] Adam and Eve were mourning about their situation, and the devil was jumping for joy because of his accomplishment.

"Let's avoid, my brothers, the sickness of envy, which is against God, the mother of homicide, the overturn of nature, the despise of affinity, the irrational trouble."[110]

---

[109] Funerary Service Hymn, pp. 206 – 207
[110] Basil the Great, About Envy, 5. P.G. 31, 380

6. Demonic Power[111]

An old lady told me: *"I'm from a village. Whoever I met, something bad happened to them. If they were on a tree, they fell and hurt themselves. They kicked me out of the village, and I cannot go back".* When I told her: *"God, please forgive them,"* she replied: *"I can't! Something is dissuading me!"*

St Basil (the Great) says that in his area, there were envious people that would hurt you even by looking at you. If you had health, beauty, youth, you could wither, become sick, or thin as a skeleton. As if they had had the power to do all these with their eyes. *"I do not accept this explanation,"* says the Saint.

He accepts another one: *"such an evil thing could be done, but not with the eyes of the human, but the devil's through the envious person."* The saint reprimands the envious: *"are you not horrified by becoming the devil's weapon? Are you not horrified by becoming the enemy of innocent people? Are you not horrified by becoming God's enemy?"*

"Do not eat the bread of a miser, Nor desire his delicacies" (Prov. 23:6), St Basil (the Great) having this in mind advises us to stay away from en-

---

[111] Basil the Great, About Envy 4. P.G. 31, 377- 380

vious people. They are dangerous! He says: *"We keep the combustible material away from the fire. Thus, we have to act similarly ourselves. We should keep away from the envious because, for them, we are combustible material."*

However, no matter how far you stay, you keep being in danger. E.g., two envious people discuss (with envy) all the good things you have. This way, they open the door to the devil (who waits just outside) to come in (through their envy) and hurt innocent people!

In these cases, our Church has a special prayer. *"O Lord Our God, the King of the ages, almighty and all-powerful, (...) the physician and healer of our souls; the security of those who hope in you; we pray to you and beseech you: Remove, drive away and banish every diabolical activity, every satanic attack and every plot, evil curiosity, and injury, and the evil eye of mischievous and wicked men from your servant."* [112]

---

[112] Prayer against the evil eye, by Basil the Great from the church book "Euchologion"

In urgent and serious cases, this could be read as part of an exorcism[113].

---

[113] The envious men can be the devil's instruments, but this does not mean that the devil can do what he wants in this world. Alas...! He cannot do anything of his own accord. To sift the disciples of Christ, he asked permission from Him. The Lord said, *"Simon, Simon, behold, Satan hath desired to have you, that he may sift you as wheat"* (Lk. 22:31). Christ did not allow the devil to do so. In order to hurt Job, he needed to seek permission from the Lord (Job 2:2). And the Lord allows temptation, according to our resistance (1 Cor. 10:13). (More in the book: Confronting the Devil. Magic and the Occult. 2nd Revised Edition. "Archangels Publication", 2019).

The Prophet Samuel

7. When They Envy Us

We are also tested in front of the eyes of God. We should confront the enemy as God wishes, to forgive him, to love him, pray for him, and not let hatred control us.

When our enemy sees our kindness and our love, he might come to his senses unless his viciousness can be cured with no human medication as it happened in the case of scribes and Pharisees. They were so vicious that they could not even be cured by Christ! They did not beat envy not because they were not able to, but because they did not want to.

But envious people are not all vicious like the scribes and Pharisees. There are exceptions. With the right way, they could be "reanimated" like king Saul. Thanks to David's kindness, he came to his senses and loved David. Briefly:

Saul's troops chased David, and he was hidden in a cave. Saul went into the same cave to spend the night! He was sleeping. David let him sleep! Saul woke up without realizing that David was there! When he went out of the cave, David shouted him. *"My lord, the king!"* (1 Sam. 24:8) Saul turned back. He was caught by surprise!

David bowed in front of him (because he was the king) and said to Saul: *"Why do you listen to the words of men who say, 'Indeed David seeks your harm'?"* (1 Sam. 24:9). In reality, it was Saul that wanted to kill David. *"He said that in order to be in a better position. That somehow, Saul was innocent, and the others were guilty. He wanted to have a proper conversation with him".*[114] David explained to him that if he really wanted to kill him, he would have done it that day in the cave! *"But my eye spared you, and I said: I will not stretch out my hand against my lord, for he is the Lord's anointed"* (1 Sam. 24:10), and he promised: *"But my hand shall not be against you"* (1 Sam. 24:12). That was it!

Saul was astonished! He said to David crying: *"And you have shown this day how you have dealt well with me; for when the Lord delivered me into your hand, you did not kill me. For if a man finds his enemy, will he let him get away safely? Therefore may the Lord reward you with good for what you have done to me this day"* (1 Sam. 24:18-19). And by seeing his attitude and the protection he had from God, he understood that the moment

---

[114] John Chrysostom, Homily 2nd ,3 on David & Saul, P.G. 54: 691-2

had come for God to reward him, to take his place and become a king.[115]

"And now I know indeed that you shall surely be king, and that the kingdom of Israel shall be established in your hand. Therefore swear now to me by the Lord that you will not cut off my descendants after me, and that you will not destroy my name from my father's house. So David swore to Saul. And Saul went home" (1 Sam. 24:20-22), And David kept his oath.

Something similar happened to Joseph. (Remember: His brothers envied him!). Thanks to his kindness, God acted from behind the scene and proclaimed him king of Egypt! (Gen. 41:44-46)

---

[115] John Chrysostom, Homily 3rd, ,8 on David and Saul.P.G. 54, 707

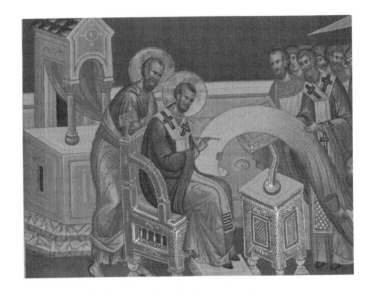

St Paul guiding St John Chrysostom

8. Against Envy [116]

"Let us not become conceited, provoking one another, envying one another" (Gal. 5:26). Since vanity produces envy, then in order for the envy to disappear, we have to be cured of our vanity. St Basil (the Great) gives us the right recipe:

"For the Christian, everything belongs to the earth; ranks are vain.[117] They do not have 'eternal' in them. If they are used properly, they can become means in order to acquire eternity, but if they are used improperly, they can become the weapons for our eternal condemnation. By themselves, they do not save or condemn us. If you see earthly things under this scope, you will not have any envy in you.

---

[116] Basil the Great, about envy, 5 P.G. 31, 381-5

[117] Vanity of vanities, says the Preacher; *"Vanity of vanities, all is vanity"* (Eccl. 1:2), said the famous King Solomon. And people are sacrificed for these vain things. *"The little kids think that their toys are great! But that does not mean that their toys are really great. Their inevitable judgment sees them as great. Something analogous also happens to those who admire earthly glory and vain things. That is to say, they themselves consider these things as great, but it does not mean that they are really great. Proof, that they have a childish mind!"* (St John Chrysostom, Homily on Psalm 142. P.G. 55, 450-451).

It is possible that someone has money, land, and they do not keep them for themselves but distribute them to the poor. As long as they serve virtue and the common good, they deserve to be glorified and loved. How can you envy such a person? If someone has the gift of eloquence and benefits the church, will you envy them?

What do you do when the sun spreads its beams? Do you envy it for doing so? Do you close your eyes, so you do not see it? Of course not! You enjoy its light. You have to act similarly when someone is eloquent and uses their gift to enlighten souls at the church. Unless you wish that both he who is benefited and he who listens to them and admires them disappear. How would you be forgiven at the final judgment?

However, when man uses his gifts in a wrong way, to his loss, he is similar to the soldier who has his sword in order to fight the enemy in the war, and he turns it against himself instead. This soldier deserves pity, not envy. He fights to destroy himself."

Abba Isaiah says: "if a man acquires a utensil and he does not use it when he needs it would be as if he has never acquired it." [118]

---

[118] Evergetinos, v. 4. Case 16. Abba Isaiah 1,1

If the mind that God gave to you remains unused, it would be better not to have it.

Christ healing the sick

EPILOGUE

1. Passions and Illnesses

"*When a sick person approaches us, he explains his sickness to us and seeks a cure. But he does not tell us about all the things that have to be corrected in his life, like his sins, his passions, etc. Remember: passions, hatred, envy, etc. are a wound on our benevolent nature and have consequences on the health of our soul and body.*" [119]

"You gave me stomach-aches," "my blood pressure has risen because of you," "my heart broke," we tend to say when someone tortures us with their behavior. Just like a doctor told me, all this is true.

The body does not become sick only from microbes or the pollution of the environment, cold or bad nutritional habits, but also from the condition of our soul. For example, the first factor to blame for heart diseases is stress!

Similarly, what can be harmful to the body are the passions of the soul, e.g., anger. "*five minutes of suppressed rage have a negative effect*

---

[119] Paul Tournier, The Healing of Persons, Harpel and Row pub. New York, 1965, p. 4-5.

on the immune system" Dr. Ioannis Boukovinas recently claimed.

Chronic hatred is also harmful to our health. According to research by a team of American scientists: *"people who keep thinking about how others hurt them are at risk of long-term stress, depression, psychosis, hypertension, and heart disease."* [120]

The passion of envy can be equally harmful. *"The evilness we keep inside makes our organism produce a poisonous hormone that can be the cause of many diseases!"* a psychiatrist said.

If the passions (hatred, envy, etc.) make our health fade away the opposite: virtues, love, forgiveness, mildness do good to our health and can even cure diseases. A sick man that had undergone a heart operation asked his doctor: *"What should I look out for now?"*; *"Be a better version of yourself."* said the doctor.

God shouts: *"My son, do not forget my law, but let your heart keep my commands; for length of days and long life and peace they will add to you"*

---

[120] A psychologist recited to me: A mother-in-law hated her daughter-in-law. And the neck distorted, it turned back! When, with the help of the psychologist, she forgave her daughter-in-law, her neck was automatically cured! The passion of hatred "attacked" her on her neck. It could have "attacked" her anywhere else, heart, head, etc.

(Pr. 3:1-2). *"Fear the Lord and depart from evil. It will be health to your flesh, and strength to your bones"* (Pr. 3:7-8).

The Good Samaritan

2. Before the Sick

The man that was the victim of theft was beaten, wounded, abandoned in the desert naked, and was left to die (Lk. 10:30), is the man enslaved by his passions.

Who does not suffer from passions? Which mortal does not bear wounds? All of our fellow men have wounds. It has been well said: *"the inner man is full of wounds to such an extent that no matter how much you take care of it, it never heals."* As the wound on the inside is not visible.

So, how would it make you feel to see somebody being hurt and covered in blood? Would you yell at him just because he was wounded? Certainly not. You would feel sympathy. That is what a person needs who have been hurt by his passions and sins and not hatred or any other kind of attack.

"Do not look at his sin. Get over it. Think about the good deeds he has done. And you will see that he is better than you".[121] *"Do not hate the sinner because we are all the same. Hate the sin and pray for the sinner in order to look like Christ. If you*

---

[121] Basil the Great, about humility, 5. P.G. 31, 525

133

hate the sinner, you prove that you are a sinner because you do not have love.

Nevertheless, God does not reject you. Imitate as much as you can His magnanimity. Become a preacher of His naivety. Show mercy to your fellow servant and win God's sympathy through your sympathy." [122]

It is not enough to show our sympathy towards a wounded person, but we have to contribute to his cure. *"Strengthen your brethren"* (Lk. 22:32), said Christ to Peter. Imitate the good Samaritan who did everything in his power in order to cure the wounds of his fellow man who had been a victim of some thefts. (Lk. 10:33-35). And the Lord is definitely going to show us mercy.

"Christ suffered for the sinners. Thus, if you see a person who is sick, physically, or mentally, and you are by his side, you can consider yourself as a martyr for Christ's sake". [123]

---

[122] Abbas Isaac the Syrian. Evergetinos v. 2. Case 41,3.
[123] Abba Isaac the Syrian. Logos 58.

3. "Security"

"Are you afraid of death?" They asked an old monk from the Holy Mountain, and he answered: *"I'm afraid of life; of my passions....!"*

If you want to secure your house, you will have to seal all the entrances, front doors, windows, and skylights. If you seal the doors and windows and leave a skylight open, your house is not secured. There is an excellent chance to get robbed. You should lock everything!

The same thing happens to our soul. We should keep out the passions. If we leave any door open, we are in danger. Adam lost paradise just because of one passion (because of gluttony).[124] So, *"you may not be a prostitute. So what? What is the use since you are avaricious?"* [125] But of course, it is a good thing that you are not a prostitute. But to save your soul, it is not enough not to be a prostitute. The five foolish virgins

---

[124] God said to Adam and Eve: *"But of the tree of the knowledge of good and evil you shall not eat, for in the day that you eat of it you shall surely die"* (Gen. 2:17). That (says St Basil) was a commandment for fasting. And it was the first commandment that God gave to man. So fasting and mankind have the same age! (Homily1, 2 about fasting,1, 3. P.G. 31, 168).

[125] John Chrysostom, Homily 29, 4 on Acts. P.G.60, 219)

stayed out of God's Kingdom even though they were virgins. (Mt. 25:12). Imagine what would have been their destiny if they had been prostitutes. [126]

"Only by calling my brother foolish, I sin (Mt. 5:22) says St Basil the Great and continues: What is the use of keeping the rest of the commandments? What is the use of being freed from all sins if I am enslaved by one? (Jn. 8:34). What is the use of not having been sick from all the diseases but only one, which eventually will lead you to death? What is the use of all of your organs being healthy except for one? If all the commandments were not of equal importance, why to receive them anyway?"

All of them are important for our salvation. *"You should keep all the things that I have said to you"* (Mt. 28:20), said Christ to His students who were going to preach in the whole world.

---

[126] The foolish virgins had put a little oil in their lamp (Mt. 25:3), and their lamps began to extinguish (Mt. 25:8). That is to say, they had not much mercy! They were "foolish" because they could beat the major passion, namely the passion of the flesh, and they were defeated by the minor, by their stinginess! And since they were foolish they went to Hell. (St John Chrysostom, Homily 78, 1, 2, on the Gospel Matthew P.G. 58, 711, 712).

What about those Christians who keep some of the Lord's commandments? Peter, who left everything behind for Christ's sake, refused to have Christ wash his feet, Christ said to him: *"if you don't let me wash your feet, you do not belong to me" "If I do not wash you, you have no part with Me."* (Jn. 13:8). Just with a simple transgression out of respect, Peter put his place next to Christ at risk. [127]

However, we do not know if He is going to judge His servants on the same base. Because Saint Vassilios the Great, in a different speech, says: *"the Lord judges the man as a whole and not partially"* [128] He takes into account all of our deeds, not some specific ones. *"Who has known the mind of the Lord?"* (1 Cor. 2:16). His judgmental criteria are mysterious!

What we should keep, though, is that we should continuously fight, to keep all of the Lord's commandments, and obtain mercy from Him.

---

[127] St Basil the Great, Terms at Length, 1, 3. P.G. 31, 893
[128] St Basil the Great, about Humility, 5. P.G. 31, 525

"It's not who we are when we read a spiritual book
that is important, but who we are when we close it."
Monk Symeon the Athonite

4. The Seedless Tree [129]

"Every tree which does not bear good fruit is cut down and thrown into the fire" (Mt. 3:10).

"Let all bitterness, wrath, anger, clamor, and evil speaking be put away from you, with all malice. And be kind to one another, tenderhearted, forgiving one another, just as God in Christ forgave you." (Eph. 4:31-32).

With these words in his mind, St John (Chrysostom) says: *"be kind and merciful to one another," "it is not enough not to harm someone in order to enter into the Lord's Kingdom, but you should do many good deeds. The winner is the person who can be a benefactor for the city".*

It is not enough not to be angry with the fellow man; you should show virtue, unresentfulness, tolerance, goodness. You have to show virtue to your brother; love, mercy, kindness.

It is not enough not to envy our brother; we have to show him that we are happy with his progress.

"If a slave does not steal, curse, or drink, but at the same time, he does not follow his master's commandments, is he not going to be punished?

---

[129] Homily 16,1 to Ephesians. P.G. 62, 111-112

Or, a farmer who does not exploit us or steals us, but at the same time, he does not cultivate or fertilize the land. Even if he has not been unfair to anyone, he deserves to be punished. What if the mouth does not bite the hand, but it does not fulfill its mission by refusing to eat? Wouldn't it be better to be shut?"

The lazy servant of the parable gave precisely the same amount of money as he got (Mt. 25:24), but Christ said that he was doomed anyway, *"and cast the unprofitable servant into the outer darkness. There will be weeping and gnashing of teeth."* (Mt. 25:30). Because he did not do anything to increase it. As you may see, do not only those sin who do wrong but also those who do not do any good. [130]

"Look at my hands Lord, they are sparkling clean!" said a soul to God, and God replied: *"clean but empty!"*

---

[130] Homily 88,3 on the Gospel of Matthew 3. P.G. 58, 214

5. Our "Character"

St. John Chrysostom says that our character is shaped even by the experiences we acquired in our infancy! [131] That is remarkable because it was said by a saint monk who lived in the 6th century! It is also remarkable that modern science says that our character is more influenced by the environment we are born into and raised in than by heredity![132]

Let's suppose that two brothers inherited some land from their father, 0.5 acres each. However, the first's land was "difficult" to cultivate,

---

[131] Step 26, On discernment of thoughts, passions and virtues, 22

[132] Different character, different conscience! The conscience is valid, when it has been formed, according to the Gospel, and not according to the world. However, today, the world creates "new" consciences. *"I feel guilty because I killed a rat."* This was told to me by an old lady in confession, while in the old days she had killed cats, rats etc without any guilt! So the materialists who say that there is no innate conscience are right? We know that stealing is bad. However, who taught us this? If they had not told us this, when we steal from the orphans, would we feel wonderful? So, there is innate conscience which tells us that stealing is a sin. And *"if you want something do not regard it as a sin, do it many times"*, because this kills conscience and guilt!

full of rocks and rough soil. The two brothers cultivated their land, seeding wheat.

He who had inherited the infertile earth worked really hard; he got rid of the stones, dug to smoothen the soil, and then he seeded it. He collected the same crop as his brother. However, we admired the first brother who turned the infertile soil to a fertile one. Even if his crop were less, he would still be admirable.

Something similar happens with the character we inherit.

Some are born obnoxious and intolerant, and others mild and calm. God will judge these two differently based on their characters.

Some are born hateful and vicious, and others good and peaceful. The first has to fight a long way compared to the second one to "beat" his difficult character and reach the second person's level who by nature is good. In this case, as well, God will judge the first who was hit by hatred and the second one who was born good but was also hit by hatred in a different way!

Some are born with a jealous nature, and some are not capable of jealousy—same case. The first has to fight constantly compared to the second one to beat jealousy and reach the state of the second person. And again, God will differently judge the first who was hit by jealousy and the second one who, although had no jealousy in him, became a slave of it!

For God, two things count the most: our personal character and the fight we give against our character. Every person should get their reward based on their work, *"each one will receive his own reward according to his own labor."* (1 Cor. 3:8).

St Paisios the Hagiorite: *"We should not brag about our virtues, and we should not be disappointed if we have flaws. The good God will take into account the fight that everybody gives regarding their character and passions".*

We should not be so confident about our judgments because we will be surprised on the day of our judgment!

The Transfiguration of Jesus Christ

6. Passions and Holy Grace

"What does human mean?" They asked a hermit monk. *"A bag full of passions and weaknesses!"* The hermit replied. Our challenge: To empty the bag first and then to fill it with Holy Spirit!

The holy fathers speak from their ascetical experience: *"you have to give your blood to receive the Holy Spirit."* As long as we remain, slaves of our passions, we do not fulfill the requirements to receive the grace of the Holy Spirit. We do not even fulfill the requirements to sense the fatal consequences of our sins! Because our soul is already dead; it has been blackened because of the action of the passions.[133]

---

[133] Come now, with such a black soul, to analyze the Holy Bible and to teach the world! *"And an evil man out of the evil treasure brings forth evil things"* (Mt. 12:35). As shepherds, we have to think that we say to the people they do not "express" God, but ourselves! We "mix up" the word of God with our passions, and we offer this "mixture" to the hungry people. The Lord "complains" to us: *"They* (His sheep) *eat what you have trampled with your feet, and they drink what you have fouled with your feet"* (Ez. 34:19) Sometimes it is better not to talk ...!

When a drop of ink is spilled on a black gown, it is not visible; when it is spilled on some white surface, it is visible. When the black ink of sin drops onto our black soul, our soul cannot realize the blackness because they both have identical colors. But, when our soul gets cleansed and becomes bright white, it is easy to sense blackness and do everything to avoid it.

St Seraphim of Sarov, being a human, committed an offense. His bishop wanted to make him the leader of a monastery, but he refused; he disobeyed. And he felt the blackness of his sin! It was such an unbearable feeling that for three whole years, he stayed on a rock begging the Lord to have mercy on him and cleanse him from the pollutant of sin.

When you have a child, and you lose it, you realize what the loss of a child means—mourning and crying. And when you have obtained the holy grace, and you lose it, you realize what the loss of the holy grace means.

For this reason, whoever obtained the holy grace worries about how to protect it from the barbarous invasion of passions. And they constantly keep supervising the movements of these barbarians. E.g., when a (visitor) monk started to talk to St Poemen for subjects regarding Heaven and spirit, the great Saint began to feel uncomfortable and turned his head away. When the monk began to speak about passions, the Saint was relieved and voluntarily accepted to have a discussion with him![134]

All we do is nourish our "enemies," and as a consequence, we distance ourselves from the Lord! *"If we do not beat our passions, we came to this world in vain! We probably came for some evil reason; for our self-destruction...!"* [135]

As long as we are alive, there is a chance of salvation. (We should pity those who died and went to Hell!). Trying is enough. And through the Lord's grace, everything is possible. AMEN.

---

[134] Gerontiko. Abbas Poimen, 8
[135] John Chrysostom, Homily 84, 3 on the Gospel of John P.G. 59, 458

Made in the USA
Middletown, DE
20 June 2021